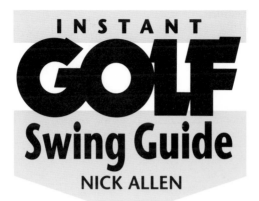

INSTANT
GOLF
Swing Guide

NICK ALLEN

THE SWING GUIDE

First published in 1992 by
Ashford, Buchan & Enright
31 Bridge Street, Leatherhead, Surrey

British Library Cataloguing in Publication Data

Allen, Nick
Instant Golf Swing Guide
I. Title
796.352

ISBN 1-85253-271-8

Designed and produced by
SP Creative Design
Linden House, Kings Road, Bury St Edmunds, Suffolk
Art Director: Rolando Ugolini
Editor: Heather Thomas
Photographs: Rolando Ugolini

The publishers would like to thank Greg Dukart,
Head Professional at East Sussex National Golf Club
for his help and allowing us to take photographs
at the course.

Typeset by Halcyon Type & Design, Ipswich, Suffolk
Origination by Graphicolour, Thurston, Suffolk
Printed and bound in Great Britain by The Bath Press,
Bath, Avon.

Contents

The author

Nick Allen is a PGA Professional and consultant with Apollo Golf Shafts, which operates a Tour Support Service on the European Tour. He has played extensively on the professional circuit both in the United States and Europe. He is also the director of a golf course development company. Nick Allen lives in Kent, England.

CHAPTER ONE

The set up

The address position forms the foundation on which a sound golf swing is built. Rarely will you see a player who has a sound swing, address the ball poorly. Although varied theories of swing technique have evolved, pictures that show golfers dating back as early as the mid-eighteenth century indicate similarities in the address position to those that are still taught today.

You will discover how much the set up can influence your game; in fact, many swing faults can be traced back to a problem in the set up. Establishing a sound address position will act as the catalyst towards unlimited improvement with your own golf swing.

Checking your grip

The most popular grip used today is the Vardon, or overlapping grip, named after Harry Vardon. Its role in controlling the club face throughout the swing is universally accepted. To build the grip, you should follow the instructions outlined here.

1 Set the club face aiming along the intended target line (below left). Hold the butt end of the club between the thumb and forefinger of the right hand; this ensures the stability of the club face during left hand placement. Place the palm of your left hand (below, inset) against

the left side of the grip which lies across the middle joint of your first finger with the butt end of the grip supported underneath the pad on the left palm.

2 Maintain your right forefinger/thumb grip and close the left hand with your thumb positioned slightly to the right of centre (as viewed from the playing position).

3 Lift the club to waist height ensuring that the line formed between the thumb and forefinger points between the chin and right shoulder. There must not be a gap between the thumb and the first finger. You should feel that your forefinger is

common fault with right hand placement is the palm-based grip resulting from incorrect positioning of the small finger. With the standard overlapping grip, the player will often extend the small finger too far, thereby pushing the grip into the palm (as below).

'triggering' on the underside of the grip, and that your thumb is 'short' and not extended down the grip. This relationship is *crucial* for right hand placement.

4 It is essential to grip the club in the fingers of the right hand. However, the most

THE SWING GUIDE

5 It is crucial that you feel the first joint extend (below left) just beyond the knuckle of the forefinger as this achieves the 'finger' placement (bottom left).

method of right hand placement. Beware! Do not push the small finger through fully, as this again bases the grip in the palm (below and bottom right).

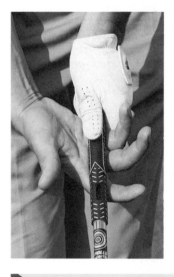

6 If you are unable to achieve this position with comfort, it is possible that your palm and finger size are more conducive to the interlock

7 Feel the underside of the grip sitting between the middle and end joint (below); this will allow you to achieve the vital finger position.

8 Lift the club into an upright position and rest it on your right shoulder (below) to check how you have established the overlap/interlock position.

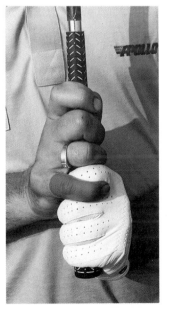

9 At waist height, check the lines meeting at a point between the chin and right shoulder. Feel how your left thumb is secured under your right pad, your right thumb positioned left of centre with your first finger forming the trigger position very slightly extended (above).

Stance and posture

Grip, stance and posture, ball position and alignment make up the elements in the address position that provide the foundation for the swing. A vital correlation exists between these elements, each one being of equal importance. Correct stance and posture form the basis for the correct body turn, swing path, and swing plane.

1 The angle formed between your trunk and lower body is vital. Frequently golfers are advised: "Bend your knees, imagine you are sitting down" but this can promote an incorrect posture and also create swing problems (inset).

2 The ideal posture when viewed from behind will result in a right angle or 'T' being formed by the shaft of the club and the upper body, giving the appearance that the player is sitting back to find the seat (below).

Practice drill

1 Place your feet shoulder width apart, flex your knees with your trunk in an upright position, look straight ahead and extend your arms with the club shaft parallel to the ground (below).

2 Without moving your arms, slowly bend forwards from the waist while maintaining your knee flex (below).

3 The head should be centred with the hands slightly leading the club head, giving the impression of a straight line formed between your left arm and the club shaft. Allow the weight of the club to pull your arms to a natural extension – do *not* lock them at the elbows. The insides of both feet are shoulder width apart; the right foot is set at right angles to the target line with the left foot turned slightly outwards (below).

The weight is evenly distributed between your left and right legs. The correct posture and distance from the ball will 'pull' the centre of gravity down towards your feet and through towards the balls of the feet.

Ball position

Each club in your set contains a graduated club face loft designed to produce shots of varying height and distance. Swing speed, plane, path and angle of attack are influential in this process. Correct ball position is a vital factor (below).

1 The driver contains the least amount of club face loft and demands a swing that passes momentarily horizontal with the ground at the bottom of its arc (bottom), progressing to an upward arc as the ball is swept away from its forward position just inside the left heel (opposite).

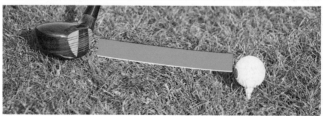

2 Conversely, the sand wedge is the shortest and most lofted club. The club head has to achieve a descending point of contact which requires the ball to be positioned more centrally. You will notice that the angle between the left arm and club shaft is retained longer during the downswing than with the driver (below).

3 As the club progressively lengthens, the need to

execute a steep angle of attack diminishes, and the ball position moves progressively forwards, inducing a sweeping action.

4 As you set up, view the position of the back of the ball in relation to the stance (below). As you look down, picture a line from the back of the ball at right angles to your stance line. Always take the line from the back of the ball because this is the part with which you make contact.

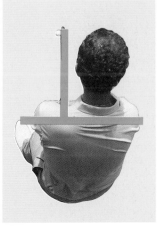

Pre-shot routine and target alignment

Target alignment creates problems for players at all levels. In fact, the majority of faults encountered by players during the set up occur through failing to adopt a sound pre-shot routine. This systematic approach to addressing the ball acts as a checklist: a countdown procedure that will lead to composure at address and prepare you to start the golf swing.

1 Standing behind the ball with the club gripped in the left hand, look down the target line and select a reference point in front of the ball that is within 12 inches (below).

2 Approach the ball in a semi-circle (below) and take up your usual pre-stance position opposite the ball.

3 Lift the club to waist height (below) and position the right hand.

4 Take a short step forwards which positions your right foot slightly behind the ball, at right angles to, and parallel with, the target line. Simultaneously bend forwards from the waist and ground the club (right).

5 As you look down from the playing position, before you commit the placement of your left foot make sure that an imaginary line crosses your right toe, hips and shoulders, parallel with the target line (below). You can determine this by visualizing a line from the ball to your reference point and setting the right foot and shoulder line accordingly.

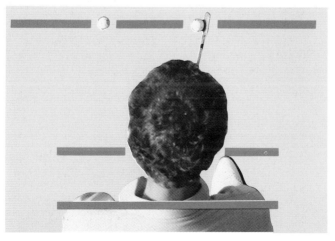

6 Position the left foot according to the appropriate ball position and widen the right foot accordingly (as shown in this sequence).

Summary

The pre-shot routine accounts for the vital factors essential in the set up.

1 Establish the left hand placement, shot visualization, and target line reference.

2 Assume the important pre-stance position; time for further visualization

and concentration.

3 Establish the right hand placement and an overview and 'feel' for grip.

4 and **5** Establish your posture, distance from the ball and alignment.

6 Take up your stance and ball position.

CHAPTER TWO

The swing

Starting the swing and club head path

Starting the swing from an impulse response leads to inconsistency. This is usually associated with golfers who do not have a clear understanding of how the swing should start. Acquire a clear concept and you can control the initial move consciously.

1 At the very point that the swing unit commences motion, the left side of the body responds in absolute unison starting a pivotal turn (below); emphasis is placed on the unity of this initial move. Immediately before starting, focus on something to press the 'start button'.

THE SWING GUIDE

2 The start button is the left hand initiating the swing motion (left) by pushing the club head away from the ball. Sound fundamentals at address linked to a sound start will influence the correct change in club face position during the takeaway; do *not* influence this with the hands. (See the club face control drill in your backswing checklist on page 24.)

3 As the club reaches a horizontal position, the shaft should be parallel with your target line, with the back of your left hand, and the club face at the same angle (below). The pivotal turn from the hips will pull the left knee inwards while the right knee retains its flexed position.

Body turn

Here we can see the correlation between the turning motion in the swing and the set up. A good backswing turn is based on the correct posture at address. The turn serves two functions: it allows the hands and arms a wide uninhibited swing arc; and it is also a contributing power source to the swing.

1 Imagine that you have taken your set up with a revolving tube placed around your trunk (above). As the swing starts, you cannot move laterally; the left side of the body commences a pivotal-circular movement in time with the motion of the swing unit. As the backswing progresses beyond the midway point the trunk and

shoulders continue to turn whereas the hips would have resisted somewhat (above) to turn through approximately 45 degrees.

> **Caution:** There are two functions in the turn that are reaction responses and not conscious moves:
>
> ● The left knee response.
>
> ● The resistance created between the 90 degree shoulder turn and the 45 degree hip turn.

2 A view from this angle shows the plane on which the shoulders turn. It could not be horizontal unless the trunk was upright during the address position (below). It should not be at this steep angle which is actually a shoulder tilt (below) and a common problem with many players. It is midway between the two and revolves around the axis through the shoulders which was formed at address (bottom).

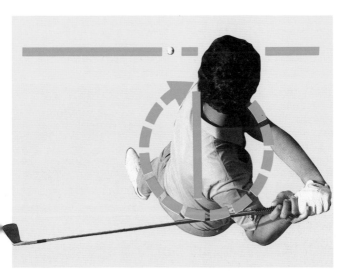

3 When viewed from above (top and above), the pivotal-circular motion is emphasised, with a clear indication of the swing path resulting from the influence of a correct set up and turn. At the top of the swing the body has turned fully with the shoulders at 90 degrees. The power source from the turn functions as an automatic recoiling process created by the winding resistance during the backswing.

From takeaway to backswing completion

During the backswing, as the swing unit progresses towards hip height, an important process takes place which is a contributing power source during the downswing. The way you control this process will affect recovery and subsequent contact with the ball. The wrist set during the backswing forms an angle between the left arm and club shaft. In the full swing, the wrists will *begin to set* as the hands approach hip height, and this is a gradual process.

1 The effect of trying to set the wrists at a specific point is one of rigidity, manufacturing a move that is not conducive to your swing (left).

2 When performed correctly it is a gradual 'set' where the wrist break blends in during the motion of the backswing (above and opposite). The width of arc is established during the takeaway, and, as the hands approach hip height, the set begins and blends in with the swing motion as the trunk continues turning and the arms swing upwards. When the shoulders have turned through 90 degrees, you have completed the backswing.

Backswing swing path and checklist

The following backswing checklist can be used during practice as a reference guide to some key factors. Use it on the practice tee or at home in front of a mirror to check the various positions. Practise the **club face control drill** to enhance your awareness of club face position during the swing.

Club face controll drill

1 At slow motion speed, start the swing and stop early during the takeaway (below).

2 Turn clockwise to readjust your set up and ground the club (opposite); if the club face

is parallel to the target line, it is square and correct (far right).

The photograph below shows a closed blade and therefore the takeaway is at fault. The correct position (right) with the club face square and parallel to the target line.

3 and **4** Similarly the drill will present a closed blade to indicate a fault in the takeaway.

Mirror drill 1

Practise taking the club back to the horizontal point in the takeaway. The back of your left hand and club face should be at a similar angle with the club shaft parallel with your target line. (A mirror will help you to check these positions.)

Mirror drill 2

Return to your address position and start again (facing a mirror, or your reflection from a window). Commence in slow motion as before, but continue turning as you approach waist height and observe the gradual process of the wrist set, while continuing to turn and swing your arms upwards. Check that you have turned fully and that you have maintained your width of arc (above and opposite).

Balance and weight distribution

1 Start another practice swing, and this time focus on maintaining your balance by placing a club on the ground as a reference point reflected in the mirror. Feel during the backswing that you are turning around the axis formed by the club. During this process, and at the top of the backswing, a subtle move will position a greater proportion of weight onto your right side; although again beware! This is not a conscious move but a reaction response.

that you retain the flex in your right knee. At the top of your swing, check that the club shaft is parallel with your target line, with the back of your left hand and club face at the same angle. The upper body angle has been retained fully throughout the backswing.

2 Take your address looking back into a mirror and, during the process of the backswing, check that the turn at the start influences the swing path to move from target line to inside. During the backswing, make sure

The start of the downswing

A good width of arc on the backswing linked to a strong turn will influence a good starting move on the downswing. The initial move down reacts, merging together with the completion of the backswing.

1 The two merge together as a result of the resistance created by the left hand pulling (below).

3 This process 'times' the motion of your hands and arms with the lower body, which is progressively transferring weight as the hips begin to unwind.

4 The *authority* given to the

created between the lower and upper body during the backswing. Do not consciously try and perform this initial move; it is a reaction response to a sound backswing turn (above).

2 Your initial 'feel' is a smooth lateral drive with the legs simultaneous with leverage

left hand is vital. The *pull* retains the angle of attack which progressively recovers as the wrists uncock. The left hand begins to rotate, squaring the face as it continues to *pull* the club head, descending (opposite top left) to *squeeze* the ball between club face and turf at impact (opposite top right).

5 The function of the left hand *pull* also serves to retain the plane and path of the downswing (right).

Impact and proper contact

Solid ball striking requires an ability during the downswing to adapt the speed and recovery of the angle between the left arm and club shaft; this will depend on the particular shot. Here we will examine a standard 5 iron shot where the ball is positioned left of centre in the stance.

1 The process of striking an iron shot requires the ball to be *squeezed* between the club face and turf at contact as the club head continues its descent towards the bottom of its arc. To achieve this, your 'feel' process is to strike downwards on to the back of the ball (below).

Remember that a divot is taken as the club

continues towards the bottom of its arc. Before the leading edge of the club head cuts the turf the ball is already in flight.

The first mark indicates the ball contact point (left). The second mark is where the club head cuts the turf, but before this happens the ball is already in flight.

2 Therefore the sequence of events that takes place at impact is as follows: club face on to the ball (*squeeze*); and then the turf. Do not consciously think about taking a divot.

3 The extent to which you feel the club head descend will depend on the playing conditions, i.e. a steeper descent to achieve a ball/turf sequence (above and above right), or a slightly more shallow angle of attack to nip the ball from a grassy lie (below and right).

Swing plane and follow through foot action

Here we shall dispel some of the misconceptions that still exist regarding the swing arc and follow through.

1 Some beginners have misconceptions about the path that the club should follow during the swing. It is common to see a player at the start of the backswing guiding the club as wide as possible along the target line; similarly on the follow through, creating a contrived swing path extending down the target line.

2 This would only be valid if we addressed the ball standing on the target line where we would have to assume an upright posture (below left).

3 The nature of your posture in a correct set up, and the principle of alignment that sets your club head and stance on to separate parallel lines, both serve to influence the turning motion of the swing which influences the swing path and plane (below).

4 You can see that although the club head starts away on the target line, it moves inside quite early as the turning motion of the body progresses (below).

5 Just after impact the club head and arms extend along the target line until the continued unwinding of the body's left side and the pivotal turn of the shoulders pull the swing back inside the target line (above).

6 As the left side unwinds and the weight transfer progresses, it begins to pull your right foot counterclockwise on to its toe (below).

7 As the arms extend into the follow through (above), the right foot has turned completely on its toes, a reaction response.

8 The arms swing through and begin to fold and, as the trunk and shoulders slow, the hands finish to the side of the head (below).

Timing and tempo

The definition of timing as it relates to the golf swing is that each swing component functions in the correct sequence during the motion of the swing (correct sequential movement). Swing timing is interrelated with tempo, which refers to the speed of the swing.

Many factors will directly affect timing and tempo, and may subsequently affect the result of the shot.

1 The majority of players swing the club too fast. This can happen simply because they deliberately want to hit the ball hard. Sometimes it can be caused by poor swing movements leading to mistiming. For example, the player with a short restricted swing resulting from a poor turn, or a strong grip with too much tension, may be forced to swing too fast (below).

2 The speed of swing motion

allows no room or time for the correct sequence of movement. Conversely some players with sound technique swing the club too slowly, consciously trying to perfect the movement.

3 A slow deliberate swing will not generate a fluidity to allow correct sequential movement. Search for an acceptable compromise between the two.

4 It will help if you are relaxed at address, so allow the weight of the club to pull your arms to a natural extension (below). Relax your shoulders and squeeze the club in the left hand as opposed to gripping tightly with the right hand. Avoid starting the swing from a cold position; waggle the club and introduce an element of movement at address, i.e. look at the target, and take some light steps to attain position.

Downswing checklist

1 Opposite a mirror or your reflection in a window, place a club on the ground as a reference for ball position; ground your club just beyond the 'butt' which indicates the ball point. Swing to the top of the backswing and stop. Simulate the downswing (below): start slowly by pulling with your left hand in unison with the initial lower body response, and stop at waist height.

2 As you continue, 'feel' the angle begin to recover (above right) while your left hip unwinds. As the club simulates the impact position, 'feel' how your body is still 'centred'.

3 From the top of the backswing, looking back at the reflection (below), start the initial move to 'feel' how the left hand leverage controls the downswing plane and path.

Ball contact drill

Take an old piece of carpet or mat large enough to swing on. Facing the mirror, mark a ball reference point and make a half backswing. Swing down 'feeling' impact in line with the ball point; the club will 'bounce' off the carpet. Restrict the throughswing, allowing it to merge with the backswing of the following swing (continual swing exercise). The drill will enhance your feel for ball striking, and a 'feel' for the uncocking of the wrists. Start to look into the mirror as you make contact, and observe the recovery of the *line* between the left arm and club shaft at impact. Gradually increase the length of swing and fully incorporate the entire sequence of movement.

Throughswing exercise

Set up normally with your left side facing the mirror. Now alter your set up to simulate an impact position. Slowly extend the throughswing, observing in the mirror how the progressive unwinding and pivotal body turn pull the swing path back inside the target line. As the body continues to unwind and straighten, the arms fold with the hands positioned to the side of the head.

Swing speed warm-up drill

A warm-up exercise and a 'feeler' for swing speed is to spend two minutes making full swings feeling that from the takeaway a gradual acceleration process takes place. Professionals frequently give the impression that they are not swinging fast; they feel the backswing as a means only of *positioning* the club ready for the downswing and hit. Their downswing speed accelerates reaching maximum speed just before impact – not midway through the backswing. Like them, you should progress through first, second and third gears before changing into top.

CHAPTER THREE

Fault recognition

Curing the hook

A hooked shot occurs when the club face in relation to the intended target line or swing path is closed at impact (below). Contrary to the intention of aiming right, which many golfers do to compensate for a hook, this practice accentuates the problem. From a closed stance position, one of two reactions usually takes place.

1 At the top of the swing the player who consciously aims right 'switches loyalty', and attempts to re-route the downswing path by 'spinning' the shoulders, creating the pull-hook.

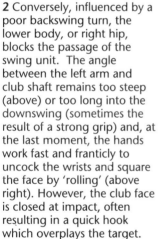

2 Conversely, influenced by a poor backswing turn, the lower body, or right hip, blocks the passage of the swing unit. The angle between the left arm and club shaft remains too steep (above) or too long into the downswing (sometimes the result of a strong grip) and, at the last moment, the hands work fast and frantically to uncock the wrists and square the face by 'rolling' (above right). However, the club face is closed at impact, often resulting in a quick hook which overplays the target.

3 The player who addresses the ball perfectly may still hook the ball if the correct sequence of swing move-ments is affected. This can occur from a takeaway fault related to the swing path, or the timing of the wrist set. A poor turn will also destroy correct sequential movement during the downswing,

especially the lower body restricting the passage of the swing unit (below).

3 Standing too far from the ball induces a flat swing (above) which can encourage the right side to 'spin' (right), throwing the club outside the line to start the downswing. If the hands roll the face closed during the downswing a *pull-hook* will result (opposite); alternatively, the right hip may block the passage promoting over-active hands as shown on page 43.

4 An extremely common problem is the grip. Quite often the player with a strong grip will roll the face open during the backswing hoping to counteract the inevitable hook. The extent to which the face is opened on the backswing inevitably will close it prior to impact.

Conversely, it is not unusual to see a player hook the ball with a weak grip resulting from an over-conscious-ness at the top of the swing which sets the right hand and arm into play to close the face.

Remedy checklist

1 Grip: Refer to the grip build sequence on pages 6-9 with particular emphasis on left hand positioning and the application of the small finger (overlapping or interlocking). This ensures the vital finger grip in the right hand. During practice, position the left hand first, ensuring the correct position before right hand placement.

2 Alignment: Refer to page 14. Make sure that your pre-shot routine accounts initially for the *target line reference point*.

Focus on the thought process described. At random during practice, lay two clubs down to check alignment (twin club alignment drill).

3 Path, plane and ball strike concept: Correct alignment allows the hips and shoulders to unwind, creating a passage for the path of the downswing. Practise striking and holding the point of impact. You should 'feel' as if you were going to give the *back* of the ball a *backhander* with the *back* of your left hand.

Curing the slice

The slice typically occurs (below) when the path of the downswing travels from outside the target line crossing inside this line through impact with the club face open in relation to the swing path. As with the hooked shot, problems frequently occur with grip and alignment.

1 The weak grip (below) where the right hand is 'wrapped' over too far tends to position the right arm too high, which opens the upper body (right). In some cases, the stance may also be open which accentuates the problem.

2 This set up usually influences the path to travel outside the target line early during the backswing; it also promotes a lateral hip-slide and tilt of the shoulders.

3 The right side will initiate the downswing (above and above right), forcing the left side of the body to clear early; the weight frequently remains on the right side throughout the entire swing.

4 The player may aim and grip correctly yet stand too close to the ball (right). This induces a *steep* start to the swing, influencing the hips to move laterally and forcing too much weight on to the right side at the top, and, again, forcing the right side of the body to move the plane and path outside the line.

5 A reverse pivot positions too much weight onto the left side at the top of the backswing. The first reaction is often a 'spin' of the shoulders which throws the weight onto the right side and the downswing path outside the line, crossing inside through impact.

6 The weak grip quite simply nullifies the feel within the hands to control the club face (right). The player has to work very hard to square the face at contact; the result is usually unsuccessful resulting in an open face, or the over-effort frequently closes the club face.

Remedy checklist

Grip: Refer to pages 6-9. Remember that the right-hand grip can only achieve correct placement if the left hand is correct initially. Constantly check that your left hand is sufficiently turned to the right to ensure the line points between the chin and right shoulder: two to three visible knuckles will verify this.

Alignment: Refer to pages 14-15. Before you commit to left foot positioning, 'feel' that an imaginary line drawn across the right foot, the hips, and shoulders is set parallel with the target line. Check your general alignment using the twin club drill.

Backswing path and turn in unison: Refer to pages 24-26. Study the initial swing start and the relationship between the swing unit and left side of the body. It is the immediate response from the left side that establishes the swing path. Practise this if possible in front of a mirror: place a target line reference on the ground in this exercise to see the change in path.

Downswing: Refer to pages 28-29. Stop at the top, momentarily start down slowly and stop. Try to 'feel' the position of your downswing plane and the path. Greater emphasis on initiating your lower body movement will increase your awareness of retaining the downswing path and plane. Refer also to page 43 which indicates for a hook or slice fault the relationship between the lower body and the path for hands and arms during the downswing.

Curing skying

The loss of distance caused by skying the ball is particularly frustrating. However, the remedy is rather more straightforward than for many other swing faults. A common cause relates to timing the wrist set process during the swing.

1 The wrists break very early in the backswing (below) creating an angle between the left arm and club shaft that is too acute. This fault in itself contributes greatly to the problem although it often nullifies the pivotal turn as well, pulling the left shoulder downwards to tilt, which in turn slides the hips laterally.

2 On the downswing, the combination of the lower body outpacing and blocking the hands and arms, in addition to the acute angle of attack, makes recovery impossible (left) and results in the club head descending on such a steep path that a divot is sometimes taken. The ball is struck frequently from the top edge of the club face. If it is positioned too far back in the stance, the problem is often accentuated (below).

3 What causes the problem? A strong grip, which is excessive to the extent where the wrists are facing the direction of the backswing, will almost certainly break immediately.

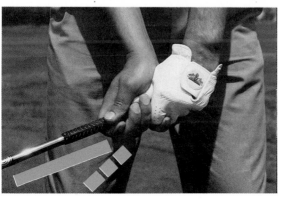

4 A player standing too close and too tall at address (opposite) will be unable to turn and establish the appropriate plane and path at the start of the swing. He will lift his arms into a steep plane (left), and during the downswing the body will very likely trap the hands and arms resulting in a steep angle of attack again (below).

5 If too much weight is positioned on the left side at the top of the backswing (below), as the hands and arms start down, the left leg often pushes the weight quickly over to the right side (bottom), and as the right shoulder drops the angle of attack steepens.

Skying: the remedy

Grip: A complete overhaul is required. If you have a particularly strong grip continually refer to all the grip preparation stages on pages 6-9.

Distance from the ball: Correct posture is inter-related with establishing the correct distance away from the ball. Check this with the drill on page 11.

Ball position: Refer to pages 12-13 regarding driver/ball position. **Note:** The short step positions the right foot slightly further behind the ball, and the left foot, when ready, slots in slightly to the left of the ball while the right 'slides' wider, thereby establishing a ball position opposite the left heel.

Swing unit and turn functioning in unison: Refer to pages 19-21 and focus on the 'start button' to initiate the swing unit. The pivotal response from your left side reacts absolutely simultaneously, and this establishes the vital swing path and plane.

The driver/ball strike concept: Refer to pages 28-29. If possible, set up in front of a mirror on the practice carpet or mat. Focus on *feeling* that through slow simulated swings your body is unwinding around a swing centre. Monitor a slightly earlier (left arm/club shaft) recovery, and feel the club pass momentarily the bottom of its arc horizontal to the ground as it progresses upwards 'sweeping' the ball.

You should also practise the **swing speed drill**. Practise this at home if possible, in front of your reflection in a window on the practice carpet or mat. Mark a position for the ball just inside the left heel. Making slow swings, observe in the reflection a slightly earlier recovery; *feel* how the club head momentarily passes horizontal with the ground and progresses on an upward arc as the ball is struck. If space allows, practise full swings *feeling* the gradual acceleration concept; use tee pegs as targets during this drill.

Curing the push

The push shot can be frustrating because quite often the ball is struck perfectly, but the initial flight is to the right of target and remains so with no flight deviation, leaving you feeling: "If only it had been on target".

1 A mis-timed sequence of movement on the downswing is sometimes a cause. The player may set up and start the swing correctly, yet before the body turn and swing length have been completed the lower body drives 'hard' towards the target (above).

2 This fast sudden move steepens the angle between the left arm and club shaft, altering the swing plane and

path. The lower body has positioned the right hip to 'block' the swing unit, not allowing the swing path to find the target line (below).

3 Quite often a simple alignment problem exists: the technique is essentially sound yet the player either does not understand the principle of alignment, or does not have a pre-shot routine that accounts for aim during the set up.

4 If the player reaches for the ball at address (right), the club will move inside the target line too early during the takeaway.

5 A swing path that moves inside the target line too soon can 'flatten' the plane (below) to the extent that the timing of correct sequential movement on the downswing is affected. The lower body again outpaces the hands and arms, 'blocking' them.

6 If the right hand dominates and 'pulls' the club away from the ball, this will move the club inside too soon.

7 To avoid hooking the ball, the player with a strong grip often attempts to counteract the hook in a number of ways. In the downswing, authority is passed over to the left hand where it nullifies any recovery between the left arm and club shaft (below), retaining an acute angle to an extent that forces the right shoulder to drop, and the weight to move back on to the right side. The result is a swing path travelling to the right of target with the left hand still resisting any recovery. It often looks as though the player is trying to 'steer' the ball. In all these examples, the inside path and flattened swing plane position the swing unit *behind* and not in *time* with the correct sequence of downswing movements.

Remedy checklist

Swing start and body turn: Refer to page 28. To trace the problem causing a premature lower body shift, focus on a tension-free smooth start to the swing, completing the body turn and allowing the initial move to occur semi-spontaneously as indicated. **Note:** The club moves away initially on the target line, so check the timing of your backswing wrist set.

Alignment: Refer back to the pre-shot routine sequence, particularly if you do not understand the principle of alignment. If you do, yet have not adopted the pre-shot routine, I suggest that this is fundamental to your improvement.

Address influencing early inside path: Refer to page 11 (distance drill). Check that you are not reaching. The weight should be *towards* the balls of the feet, not on the toes. Work on the concept of the left hand acting as your 'start button' to control the initial swing path.

Grip: Refer to pages 6-9. Your hands are the only 'feel connection' you have with the golf club, and quite simply only a fundamental grip will enable you to control the club face consistently. Moreover, the condition of the grip, good or bad, will affect other swing mechanics accordingly. Therefore you should give priority to working on your grip.

Curing toeing

Striking the ball from the toe of the club is usually associated with a downswing path that crosses inside the target line acutely just before impact. Standing too close or too far from the ball clearly relates to the problem.

1 A player standing too close, forming an upright posture, will usually swing the arms upwards into a steep plane. As the arms swing down close to the body, the trunk straightens to 'create room', and the hands and arms are pulled closer still, almost touching the body as they swing past. The path inside is so acute that the toe contacts the ball first (below).

2 Quite frequently a misconception regarding swing path distorts the turning motion, ultimately leading to a toe strike. The fault can occur even if the player is standing the correct distance from the ball, but the more common occurrence is where the player has to reach for the ball.

The club is swung 'too wide' at the start of the takeaway creating a tense contrived swing. As the arms swing upwards and the body attempts to turn, a point of resistance is reached at which the arms cannot continue, neither can the turn (which is incomplete anyway). The right side 'spins out', the path and plane move outside the line, and the weight is falling on to the right leg as the path swings acutely inside (above).

3 The same downswing
diagnosis can occur as a
result of a reverse pivot
(above). At the top of the
backswing, the weight tilts on
to the left leg, while the right
side spins to shift the weight
quickly, distorting the plane
and throwing the downswing
path outside the line again
(right).

Remedy checklist

Posture: Refer to page 11 (distance from the ball drill). The problem can occur from being too close or too far from the ball. The correct distance and posture at address will assist the establishment of a sound swing path, plane, and body turn.

Path: Refer to pages 17-21. It is vital to co-ordinate the swing unit with the turning motion during the takeaway. Practise 'focusing in' to initiate the hands and arms in unison with the turning motion.

Backswing motion: Continuing from the initial takeaway, check that you are maintaining a full width of arc and completing your turn to the top of the swing.

swings that you retain your posture, particularly the upper body angle during the downswing.

Downswing path: Refer to page 38. Facing the mirror on the practice carpet with a target line reference, 'feel' at the start of the downswing how the path and plane remain inside, and how the left hand assists this cause. Continue and check the path of the club's progression as it finds the target line approaching from slightly inside to flush with the ball.

Retain height and posture: Refer to page 38. Feel during practice

Curing the topped shot

Numerous factors contribute to topping the ball; the faults are all basic and straightforward to correct. An influential factor is a ball positioned too far forwards in relation to the particular shot in hand – standing too far from the ball will cause similar problems on the downswing. In both cases the ball simply is not where it should be when the club approaches the bottom of its arc. Essentially all topped shots occur because the club

head cannot descend to the bottom of its arc and achieve the ball/turf squeeze contact.
1 The upright posture leading to a steep swing plane will often compromise the effort to turn; the body cannot respond and the shoulders have 'underturned' at the top of the swing (opposite). The resistance the body feels at this point causes a fast 'snatch' down forcing the player up on to the toes during the downswing (below).

2 A tilt of the shoulders that forces the hips to slide laterally (this fault is often a reactive response to another fault) can tilt too much weight on to the left side (opposite top). The player progressively falls back on to the right side as the club should be attempting to descend (opposite and above) towards the ball.

An early wrist set (above) often created from an excessively strong grip can influence the left arm to collapse (left) at the top of the swing; the straightening of the left arm on the downswing is

achieved by 'casting', which forces the player on to the right side (above).

3 The topped shot frequently occurs from a deliberate effort to swing hard. The speed of the hands and arms nullifies any timing and forces the player on to the toes. Quite often the player makes a sound swing yet is simply over-anxious to see the result of the shot.

Remedy checklist

Ball position: Refer to pages 12-13 (ball positioning) and pages 14-15 (pre-shot routine). Review the concept of ball positioning and in particular the part of the pre-shot routine that accounts for it.

Distance and posture: Check your distance from the ball (see the drill on page 11). Also check your posture in a mirror. Remember that the upper body and club shaft should form a right angle. Standing tall at address causes problems; conversely, if you crouch at address you will 'straighten' out of the shot.

Grip/wrist set and turn: Refer to pages 6-9 to make sure that your grip is not too strong, as this can encourage an early set. Also, ensure that the initial start, wrist-set timing and turning concepts are correct. The start must incorporate a pivotal turn.

Swing speed: If you consciously swing fast and top the ball then clearly you need to work on modifying this aspect of your swing. Refer to the swing speed drill on page 40. The problem may be accentuated through tension, so be sure to refer to the tension-breaker pointers on pages 36-37.

Ball strike sequence: Refer to pages 30-31 regarding the ball/turf 'squeeze' concept, and then practise the ball contact drill (see page 39). Facing a mirror, mark the ball position and proceed, allowing the club to descend and 'bounce' off the ball point. Place more emphasis on the leverage from the left hand. Also practise the drills for ball contact with the driver.

Curing hitting behind the ball

Hitting behind the ball and taking too much turf is often referred to as hitting the shot 'fat', and there are a number of causes of this problem.

1 If the ball is positioned too far back in relation to the particular shot at hand, the angle between the left arm and club shaft on the downswing will not have time to recover.

2 A poor start to the swing (above) caused by either a bad grip, a misconception of the correct swing path, or simply an incorrect turn can create the steep shoulder turn and hip slide that tilt the left

shoulder, thereby positioning too much weight on to the left side at the top. As the weight shifts to the right on the downswing, the angle in-to the ball is so acute that it does not recover in time (above).

3 Mistiming the role of the turn and the swing unit during the takeaway can also encourage this problem.

Frequently golfers start the motion of the swing unit before any response from the left side (opposite). You will remember that a function of the turn is to allow the hands and arms freedom to swing and retain a good 'width of arc'. The resistance causes the left arm to collapse (inset), and in order to create some width in the downswing the hands *cast*

the club. This can cause a number of things to happen: it can force the weight forward on to the left side which 'traps' the club steep into the ball; or the body can straighten or get forced onto the right side (above and right).

4 The error combination of a strong grip and rear ball position can affect the angle of attack. Frequently these factors occur with an iron shot where the authority placed in the left hand does not allow recovery of the wrist set; the hands lead in a similar way to a cover drive in cricket.

Remedy checklist

Takeaway and wrist set: Timing the process of uncocking the wrists during the downswing requires a sound start to the swing which times this process in the backswing. It is important to initiate the left side turning immediately the club is in motion. In front of a mirror work on the wrist set. Observe the point where the set begins and 'feel' this blend in time with the backswing.

Width of arc: This is related to the points referred to above. If the takeaway and wrist set are timed correctly, and you can continue turning in unison you should achieve a good width of arc.

Grip: The ability to achieve the foregoing is based on a sound grip. Frequently a strong grip will promote this swing problem, so check your grip (see pages 6-9).

Ball position: During practice, check your ball position by placing one club across the stance, the other at right angles to the stance line. Also review the part of the pre-shot routine that accounts for ball position (see page 13).

Posture and height: Review your posture; during practice swing routines and make sure that you retain your upper body angle throughout the swing.

Curing the pull

Similar to the shot pushed right of target, a pull to the left is frustrating because the ball is often well struck. The reverse pivot is a common factor with this shot.

1 The hips will turn too freely which reverses weight back on to the left side at the top of the swing (above and right); this can occur if the club is swung inside too early which can encourage the hips to react too quickly.

2 If the right leg straightens during the takeaway this gives the hips freedom to turn excessively. The 'spin out' moves the downswing plane and swing path outside the target line, travelling across inside the line as the ball is approached. The difference between a pulled shot scenario and a slice or shank is a squaring of the club face in relation to the swing path.

3 If the swing path is excessively inside the line during the takeaway, particularly in the case of a player standing too close to the ball (above), the weight is shifted back on to the heels (below). The downswing move instinctively pushes the weight forwards towards the toes creating a loop to the downswing path (right) which throws the club outside the line. The result is the same pulled shot. In both cases, a ball positioned too far forward in the stance will contribute to the problem.

Remedy checklist

Swing path and posture: Swing path during the takeaway is inter-related with posture and distance from the ball. Therefore check that you are the correct distance away (refer to the drill on page 11). Having set up correctly, practise starting the club away on the target line – place a club on the ground as a target line reference.

Turn and right leg: In front of a mirror assume your set up and work on the turn, particularly the concept of the turn (see pages 19-21). Feel that you retain the flex in the right leg during the backswing.

Ball position: Check the ball position at random during practice: use the pre-shot routine to ensure correct positioning.

Downswing feel: Simulate a good position at the top of the swing, and slowly progress the downswing move in stages, feeling the lower body and the left hand. Retain the inside plane and path which gradually recover to slot into the target line making a 'flush' contact.

Curing the shank

The dreaded shank is a demoralizing shot because the problem often continues in spite of great efforts to correct it. The shank occurs when the ball is struck off the hosel of the iron at the heel of the club face (below).

1 A weak grip (right and opposite) where the right hand is 'wrapped' too far over the left is a common cause. The right hand will fan or roll the face open which often pulls the hips into a lateral slide as the weight favours the right side at the top of the backswing.

2 Quite often the player is very conscious that work has got to be done to square the blade. The over-effort of the right hand from the top throws the plane and path outside the line, and the right hand climbs over the left shutting the face so acutely that the hosel is rolled on to the ball (above and right).

3 Clearly, standing too close steepens the swing path which will encourage this problem. With this in mind, players often adjust their distance from the ball which flattens the swing plane, yet they do not address the problem of the grip. The same consciousness regarding the extra effort to square the face will cause the same downswing move as detailed above.

4 The combination of standing too close and a weak grip will influence the shank. The face will open in addition to a shoulder tilt and a steep swing plane. The trunk and shoulders open up early to give the swing unit some room, but the angle on to the ball is very steep and progressing inside the line.

5 It is particularly frustrating when a player grips the club and sets up well to the ball, and yet still suffers from the shank. This happens because the player does not allow the club face to position itself correctly during the takeaway. The club face is held in a closed position as the motion begins (above), while the wrists set inwards and become locked into this position for the rest of the swing (above right). An attempt to swing down the target line often presents the hosel to the ball first (right).

Standing too open restricts your turn and lays the club off. The downswing will progress acutely from outside the line to inside as per the photo sequence shown here.

Remedy checklist

Grip: Make sure that the line between your thumb and forefinger points between the chin and right shoulder (left hand). Remember also that the left hand grip dictates the positioning of the right hand.

Distance: Refer to page 11 and check your distance from the ball. During practice, feel throughout the swing that you are retaining your posture. If it changes, the swing path and plane will alter as well.

Club face position at takeaway: Review the concept of club face positioning during the takeaway, and practise the club face drill on pages 24- 25. Check your grip pressure, as it may be resisting the correct move.

Target line awareness on downswing: Many golfers attempting to avoid the shank consciously try to direct the swing path to the right of the target. This can distort the swing and, moreover, it sometimes presents the hosel to the ball first. Place a reference on the ground for the target line and another one for the ball. Looking into the mirror face on and side on, practise feeling the path and plane of downswing that enables you to progress the club head from inside on to the target line, feeling the back of the left hand and club face squared with the ball.

Curing the overswing

A position at the top of the swing where the club is horizontal is often defined as the top of backswing position. I prefer to suggest that providing the shoulders can turn through 90 degrees, the length of arc may be short of this horizontal position, particularly if flexibility restricts movement to this ideal position.

1 During the reverse pivoting movement, as the club approaches the top of the swing and the weight spins into the left side, the left arm sometimes collapses causing an overswing (below and right).

2 During the takeaway a tilting shoulder/lateral hip slide movement (right) causes the arms to lift which can also cause a left arm collapse (below).

3 A common problem occurs through tension in the set up, and this can lock the swing unit creating an excessively wide swing start. This pulls the right hip laterally, and the wrist set is delayed until very late in the backswing. When the wrists eventually do set, they sometimes cause the left arm to bend.

4 The reverse pivot allows the hips to turn too freely. If, during the takeaway, the player spins the left foot on to the toe, it allows the hips the freedom that can force the right leg to lock. The shoulders inevitably turn in excess of 90 degrees, and an overswing results (right and below).

5 If the grip of the club is not correctly positioned across the left palm, it can cause the hand to open slightly at the top of the backswing causing an overswing (below).

Remedy checklist

Grip: Check the positioning of the grip within the left hand.

Path/feet and legs/concept of turn: Concentrate on the path at the beginning of the takeaway. As the left knee is pulled inwards by the turning hip, either control the extent of heel lift, or do not lift it at all. Feel the retention of the right knee

flex. These two points are important, and you should remember the concept of the turn, with the resistance between upper and lower body acting as a control over swing length.

Wrist set timing: Observe opposite a mirror the timing of your wrist set. It is a gradual function, blending in with the motion of the backswing.

Swing technique terminology

Coil/resistance
This is achieved through a limit placed on the hip turn while the shoulders continue turning simultaneously.

Length of arc
The distance the club head travels during the backswing.

Release and recovery
An uncocking of the wrists reduces the angle on the downswing allowing the release, freeing the power created in the backswing as hands and forearms return the club face squarely to the ball. At the point of impact full **recovery** is achieved as the left arm and club shaft form a straight line.

Stationary plane
An imaginary line extending from the ball to target line, across and through the player's shoulder line at address.

Swing path
A path the club head travels on. Its position is stated in relation to the target line, i.e. inside the line; outside the line; or on the line.

Swing plane
The position of the plane is ideal if during the downswing a line from the butt end of the grip intersects the target line. If it points outside the target line, an outside-to-inside downswing path results. If it points inside the target line, an inside-to-outside swing path can result.

Target line (The line)
A straight line between the ball and target.

Tempo
The speed of the swing.

Timing
The correct sequence of movements throughout the swing.

Width of arc
The distance maintained during the swing between the hands and the body.

Wrist set
A process during the backswing that creates the angle between the left arm and club shaft.